Christa,
with much love

11/02/2012

Published by Ailsapress 2012
Port Charlotte
Isle of Islay PA48 7TS

ISBN 9780955565649

Printed by Martins the Printers
Berwick-upon-Tweed TD15 1RS

The islands of Islay and Taransay are the inspiration behind this book. They are part of the island archipelago that fringes Scotland's west coast. Islay belongs to the Inner Hebrides and Taransay to the Outer Hebrides. In these places, you are on an edge, between land and ocean, rock and sky, desolation and abundance, intimacy and awe. Time and tides come and go, concealing and revealing. The pictures have been arranged in pairs with words that seek to match a fleeting 'island moment'. With thanks to islanders, to island-lovers, to those who make cameras, and most of all to Life, for our wonderful eyes designed to receive the light.

Two limpets wait
The homing rush of ocean.

Jostling in a midden
Empty shells
That once served
The gnaw of hunger

Their only claim the stones
And peace of conscience

Direction

Dedication

Desire

Dissolution

Lifetimes

Without distraction

Fire then water
Rock then sand
Millennia in the making

Soundless
The sunlight
Swims

And blooms in our eye.

Softly softly
The water kisses
The caterpillar
caresses

Between the shadows
Lagoons of light
And a date still visible

Change
Map maker of the infinite

The mighty and the meek
Side by side

The angels are always with us
Messengers

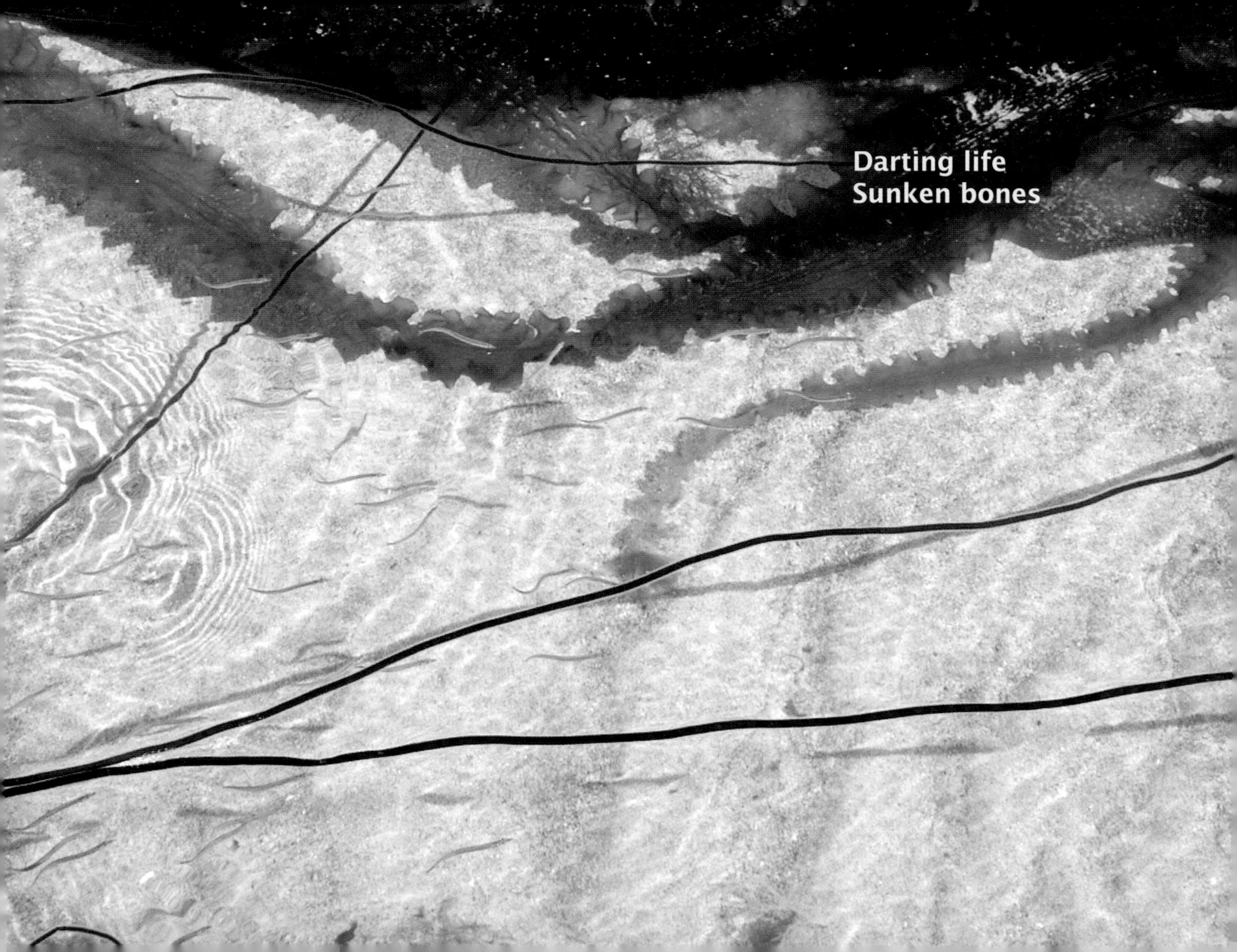

Darting life
Sunken bones

Fencing in the sand
A whim against the odds

The grace of laden grass
Bounty of the wind

Cause for wonder
We seek
Understanding

The ballast of quartz grains
In a sailing shell
Taken by the tide

LOCATIONS IN ORDER OF APPEARANCE

Cover: Islay South West from Sanaig Cliffs

Frontispiece: Taransay South towards Toe Head

Homing tide & Limpet pool: Islay by Sanaig shore

Shell middens: Taransay Paible shore

Ruin & Lintel: Taransay Tolm

Rock erosion & Orchid: Islay Sanaig cliffs

Rock waves & Seaweed: driftt: Islay by Sanaig shore

Sunlight on seaweed: Islay Lossit bay

Water over rock & caterpillar: hills of Taransay & Islay

Lagoons of light: Islay Saligo shore

Date in lichen: Taransay Loch an Duin

Rock map & Water cut: Islay Sanaig & Killinallan shores

Bird pellet: Taransay Beinn Raah

Coastline: Islay North West coast

Millie & Magpie moth: Islay by Sanaig shore & Sanaig cliffs

Sand eels & Deer skull: Islay Ardnave & Taransay by Loch Uir

Fence & Marram grass: Islay Ardnave & Killinallan shores

Seeded grass: Islay Finlaggan & Sanaig cliffs

Ruth; Marco, Sasha & Nene: Islay Sanaig cliffs

Sailing shell: Islay by Killinallan shore

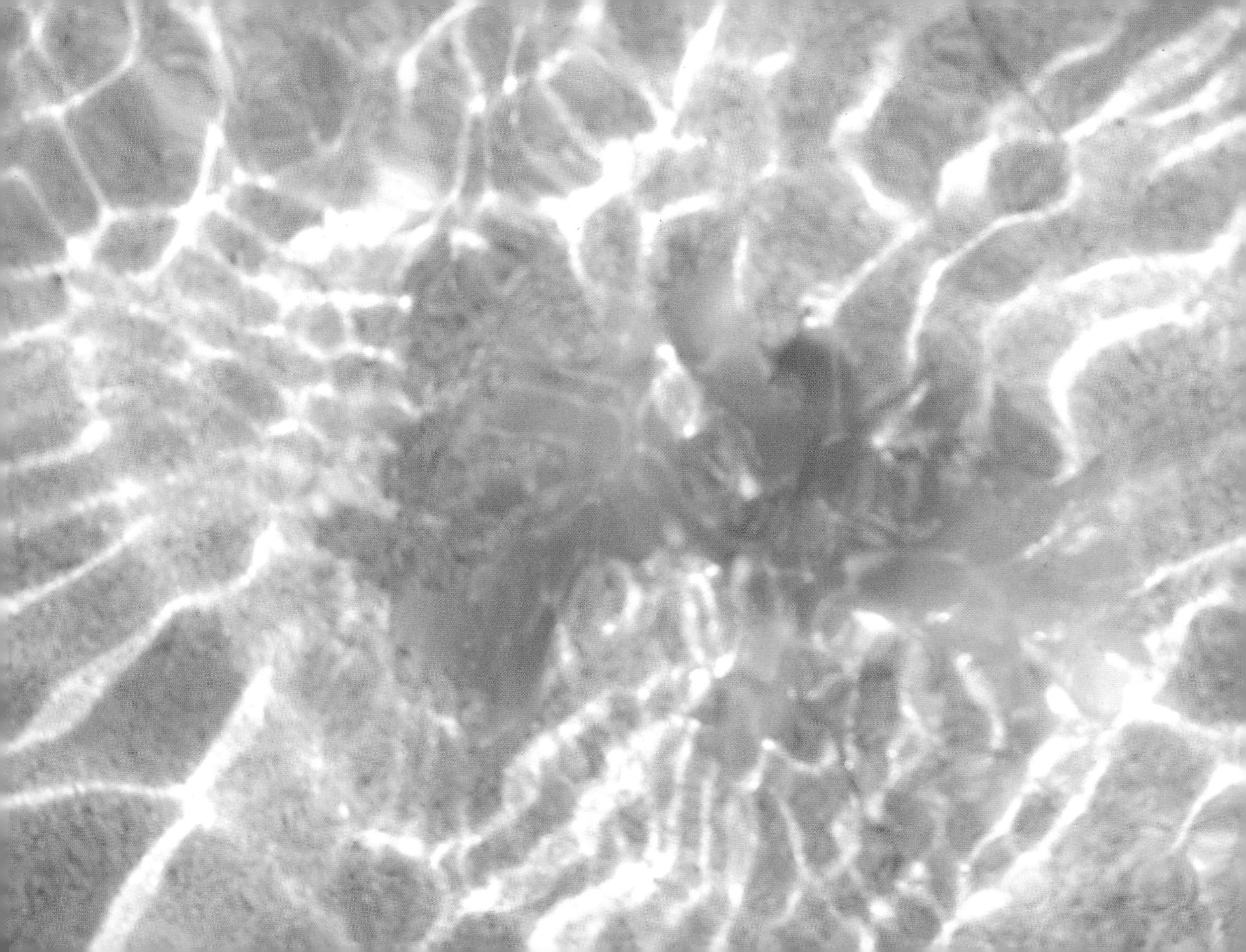